CURIOUS STORIES
OF FAMILIAR GARDEN PLANTS

By Kathy Keeler
A Wandering Botanist

AWanderingBotanist.com
Loveland, Colorado

Copyright © 2016 by Kathleen H. Keeler,
A Wandering Botanist

All rights reserved worldwide.
No part of this publication may be reproduced, distributed, or transmitted in any form or by any means, including photocopying, recording, or other electronic or mechanical methods, without the prior written permission of the publisher, except in the case of brief quotations embodied in critical reviews and certain other non-commercial uses permitted by copyright law. For permission requests, write to the publisher, addressed "Attention: Permissions Coordinator," at the address below.

Kathleen H. Keeler, A Wandering Botanist
2527 Indian Hills Drive
Loveland, Colorado 80538
www.AWanderingBotanist.com

Ordering Information:
Quantity Sales: Special discounts are available on quantity purchases by corporations, associations, and others. For details, contact the "Special Sales Department" at the address above or email Kathy@AWanderingBotanist.com

Photography: Kathleen H. Keeler

Curious Stories of Familiar Garden Plants
Kathy Keeler, A Wandering Botanist, 1st edition
ISBN 978-0-9861694-6-5

Table of Contents

Introduction..*i*

The Rise of the Tomato...1

Bachelor Buttons and Cornflowers, *Centaurea cyanus*.............11

Beautiful Blanket Flower, *Gaillardia*..............................17

Iris, All the Colors of the Rainbow................................21

Eastern Pasqueflower, *Anemone patens*, Heralding Spring....25

Orange, Oranges and Carrots 31

American Squashes..37

Colorful Columbines, *Aquilegia*..................................45

Reasons to Like Primroses, *Primula*.............................53

Snowdrops, Leading the Spring 59

The Indomitable Onion...65

Yarrow, *Achillea millefolium*, an Ancient Healing Herb..........73

Daphne, Attractive and Fragrant 81

Peas, Pescods and Pease, *Pisum sativum*........................87

Last Words..93

The plants in the garden all seem familiar, but in fact we have gathered them from all over the world over hundreds of years.

Here are some of their stories.

The Rise of the Tomato

TOMATOES ARE EVERYDAY FOODS in the United States. In fact, we often count on them to complete a salad. Years ago, on a business flight, I sat next to a vegetable-broker who told me had made a tidy profit on tomatoes one year when supplies were limited. He explained that "a salad has to have a tomato." With most vegetables, when the price gets high, restaurants substituted or did without. But since Americans felt a salad must have a slice of tomato, restaurants would pay whatever it cost for tomatoes. Knowing that, he was careful to buy tomatoes when a shortage was predicted and and happily rode the bidding war that followed.

I do not think it is quite that simple today. Restaurants have created salad options that let them omit tomatoes if they aren't affordable, but it emphasizes the stature of tomatoes in the American diet.

Thus, it seems puzzling that loving tomatoes hasn't been universal.

Tomatoes are classified as *Solanum lycopersicum*, potato family, Solanaceae. For many years they were in their own genus, *Lycopersicon*, but more recent study has determined that they are not distinct from other *Solanum* species, so they were moved into *Solanum*. That make the genus *Solanum* quite a genus. There are "1,500-2,000" species, which you can read as "lots of very similar plants." More interesting, it includes three major foods: *Solanum lycopersicum*, the tomato, *Solanum tuberosum*, the white potato and *Solanum melongena*, eggplant, aka aubergine. We eat the fruits of tomato and eggplant, and the underground tubers of potato. A few other *Solanum* species are also raised as food crops.

Tomatoes are from South America. The plant thought to be the wild ancestor of the cultivated tomato is found on the edges of the Amazon basin, for example, in Peru, in warm wet tropical conditions.

It was not grown by the Inca. Writers seem puzzled by that, but I think it reflected the environment. The Inca lived in a cool climate at high elevations. Tomatoes, even our domesticated highly-bred ones today, are not frost-tolerant: compare the consequences of the first frost on tomatoes vs cabbage or lettuce. Furthermore, they require such a long growing season that gardeners in the northern half of the United States get the seeds started indoors and transplant 4-6 week old plants outdoors after the last frost. Planting in the Andean spring, the Inca would never have gotten fruit.

In 1893 the United States Supreme Court ruled that the tomato is a vegetable not a fruit.

Experts agree that tomatoes were domesticated in Mexico. The Maya and Aztec were great farmers, growing a wide variety of plants. One of them was the tomatillo, *Physalis ixocarpa*. Tomatoes are believed to have appeared in the tomatillo fields as crop weeds.

(How they got to central Mexico from the Amazon Basin is a matter of hand-waving. "Carried by birds" is the usual answer. If you've ever seen the flocks of parrots and other fruit-eating birds that plague Central American fields, this seems pretty reasonable.)

The Maya put up with the little tomato plants in among their tomatillos, gradually starting to specifically cultivate tomatoes. By the time Cortez arrived in Mexico in 1519, the Aztecs grew a variety of different tomatoes, of different sizes and shapes.

Not only were tomatoes a late domestication by people who liked tomatillos better, they weren't eaten for themselves by the Aztecs: the Aztecs mainly used them as a minor ingredient in chili sauces.

My perception that the word tomatillo was a diminutive of tomato, so that tomatillos were named after tomatoes, turns out to be backward. The Aztec word *tomatl* names something "round and plump." Tomatillos were *miltomatl* and tomatoes *xitomatl*. The Conquistators inaccurately picked up the name *miltomatl* as the name of tomatoes. Spanish speakers reduced it to *tomate*, and English speakers said tomato.

Tomatillos were the major crop, tomatoes an afterthought, but somehow tomatoes spread across the world and tomatillos did not. When tomatoes went to Europe, Spaniards and Italians easily grew them and fairly quickly incorporated them into their cuisine.

In northern Europe, North America and Asia, however, eating tomatoes was uncommon in the 16th, 17th and 18th centuries. The problems were various. One problem was that long growing season of tomatoes. In Northern Europe and much of North America, they rarely reached the fruit stage before frost. Greenhouses and an understanding of plant biology developed steadily during the 16th and 17th centuries but could not produce very many good tomatoes.

Secondly, tomatoes could not be stored well. Even in 1800, the available preservation methods were salting, sugaring, pickling and drying. Small metal cans that could preserve food were developed in early 1800s but until the 1860s, food in cans was extremely difficult to get out (no can openers!). Home canning (affordable strong glass jars and pressure cookers, for example) became widespread much more recently. Not until the development of canned tomato sauces for home use, about 1920, was there commercial, large-scale production of tomatoes. Fresh tomatoes sold in grocery stories for home use are an even more recent development, needing rapid shipping and refrigeration. Home access was promoted by breeding tomatoes that shipped better-- reached the consumer neither crushed nor rotting--which happened at the expense of flavor, leading to the current push for better-tasting, heritage tomato varieties.

Finally, people are generally cautious about what they eat. In the 15th century, there were no *Solanum* species that Europeans routinely ate. The eggplant is from eastern Asia. It came to Arab nations in the Middle East who embraced it and shared it westward across North Africa to Moorish Spain. Christian Europe was fighting the Moors in Spain, not trading with them. The other two *Solanum* species we commonly eat, tomato and potato, are from the Americas.

In 1492, the last Moors were expelled from southern Spain and the Americas were discovered. Strange plants were available to Spanish Christians and then the rest of Europe from both places.

Next time your grocery store offers a fruit or vegetable you don't know, imagine shopping in France about 1550. The Spanish merchant has funny round vegetables for sale that you've never seen before. You don't have a clue what to call them.

Part of what happened to tomatoes is that they were introduced to northern Europe about the same time as eggplants, and confused with them. Lacking a name, merchants often called them *pomi dei Moro, pomme des Mours,* or *pomi di mori,* that is, apple (fruit) of the Moors. Which in France was heard as *pomme d'amour,* love apple.

But, probably more important, similar-looking species in Europe, for example *Solanum dulcamara,* bittersweet nightshade, *Solanum nigrum,* black nightshade, and especially deadly nightshade, belladonna, *Atropa belladonna,* are quite toxic. So the cautious European can be forgiven for not eating fruits that look so much like known poisons. The *Illustrated Flora of Britain and the Northern Europe,* 1989, writes "Nightshades *Solanum*...The fruits are generally poisonous." (p. 350) While you can read online of people all over the world eating wild *Solanum* fruits, there are over 1,000 species, some plants do have enough solanine, a toxic alkaloid, to poison you, and plant identification is difficult. Caution certainly suggests: don't eat strange relatives of belladonna.

In addition, tomatoes picked up a lot of folk tales quickly. They were thought to be an aphrodisiac, perhaps based on the name love apple. In Victorian England, knowing a fruit was an aphrodisiac was a definite reason to avoid eating it. Tomatoes also became associated with the occult, perhaps from the relationship to European relatives, especially belladonna, which was commonly linked to witchcraft, or perhaps because of the "love apple" name. In fact, the name *lycopersicum* means "wolf peach" based on the idea, widely held in Germany in the 1600s, that tomatoes were used by werewolves.

It was the end of the 19th century and well into the 20th when eating tomatoes rapidly spread through northern Europe, North America and east Asia, to take the place they currently hold as one of the best-known and most widely-eaten vegetables. We see tomatoes as very ordinary, but it has not in fact been very long since they were a novelty vegetable.

Tomatodirt.com asks: What is the difference between knowledge and wisdom?

> Knowledge is knowing that tomatoes are fruits. Wisdom is not serving them in a fruit salad.

Botanically that is correct. Fruit is a general word for structures containing seeds, from apples and grapes to pomegranates and watermelons, but also cucumbers, walnuts and tomatoes.

Every flowering plant has a fruit, though some hold only one seed (grass fruits) and others are very strangely shaped (for example devil's claw, now called double claw, *Proboscidea parviflora* of the southwestern U.S.). A very few species reproduce only through asexual buds or shoots, so the fruits abort. Tomatoes are full of seeds, but the flesh of the fruit isn't very sweet. Sweetness doesn't matter botanically: tomatoes are the fruits of the tomato plant.

HOWEVER...in the United States, tomatoes are vegetables.

Legally.

In Nix vs. Hedden 1893 the U.S. Supreme Court ruled that tomatoes are vegetables, not fruit. An importer objected to the tariff on vegetables being applied to the tomatoes he was bringing into the United States, since they were fruits. The Port Authority of New York disagreed, and the case went through appeals up to the Supreme Court. There, the justice who heard the case ruled that common American usage should prevail and that vegetables were "usually served at dinner in, with, or after the soup, fish, or meats... and not, like fruits generally, as dessert." Thus, tomatoes were vegetables not fruits.

This ruling remains in place. I enjoy the idea that tomatoes may be fruits botanically and in the rest of the world (I don't know for sure), but in the United States they are vegetables.

References:
Blamey, Marjorie and Christopher Grey-Wilson. 1989. *Illustrated Flora of Britain and the Northern Europe*. Domino Books, Ltd. London.
Coe, Sophie D. 1994. *America's First Cuisines*. University of Texas Press, Austin TX.
Couture, Lisa. 2010. The history of canning. online at scholars archive@jwu.edu
Davidson, A. 1992. Europeans' wary encounter with tomatoes, potatoes, and other New World foods. pp. 1-14 in *Chiles to Chocolates, Food the Americas Gave the World*, Nelson Foster and Linda S. Cordell, editors. University of Arizona Press, Tucson.
Morning Star. No date given. History of the Tomato. http://tinyurl.com/jypkuak
Simpson, Beryl B. and Molly C. Ogorzaly. 2014. *Plants in Our World. Economic Botany*. 4th ed. McGraw Hill Education, New York.

Bachelor Buttons and Cornflowers,
Centaurea cyanus

"CORNFLOWER?"

"What is a cornflower?"

"A bachelor button, *Centaurea cyanus* (sunflower family, Asteraceae)."

"Why would anyone call it a cornflower?"

That is a typical American reaction to the English name for the plant called bachelor buttons in the U.S.

Bachelor buttons were once weeds but they are now rare in northern Europe.

The story is this:

Bachelor buttons, the plants in the photo, are native to Europe. For all but the last 100 or 150 years, grain crops like wheat and oats were planted by people walking the fields scattering seeds, weeded by farm workers with hoes and harvested by a crew cutting the grain with sickles.

In those fields in Europe, bachelor buttons grew abundantly.

The general word for grain crops--wheat, oats, rye, barley-- in Great Britain was "corn."

When English speakers reached the Americas and saw a new grain, they called it "Indian corn." Americans have long since dropped the "Indian" and so the American grain *Zea mays* is "corn." But that is a relatively new use of the word corn.

Corn flowers were flowers that grew in the corn. The pretty blue bachelor buttons.

People turned cornflowers into garden flowers easily 400 years ago, so there are pink, purple and white ones as well as blue.

Blue remains the characteristic color, and "cornflower blue" is a recognizable shade.

The name *Centaurea* is based on a Greek myth in which the centaur Chiron, wounded by a poison arrow from the nine-headed hydra, healed himself using cornflowers on the wound. The catch is that the myth confuses two plants: cornflowers have no medicinal value. (Except perhaps as a tonic. Certainly not against poison.) It is believed that the plant in the myth was a species of gentian, specifically centaury *(Centaurium)*. The incorrect identification of the healing herb goes back to Theophrastus, 288 B.C.

Cyanus is a Greek word for dark blue. I found two quite different associated stories, first, that Cyanus was a mythological youth who loved the flowers, spent all his time making wreaths of them and died on a bed of cornflowers, so the goddess Flora named the flower after him. Alternatively, they are named for the nymph Cyane who, when Persephone was abducted by Hades, was so distraught she turned herself into a deep blue pool.

The name bachelor button also has several possible origins. First, the *Oxford English Dictionary* says a number of double round flowers were called bachelor buttons, but none of the examples given in the OED are blue or a *Centaurea*. Second, if you google "bachelor button," you can find a button that does not need sewing, suitable for bachelors who cannot use a needle and thread. Some are round and look somewhat like the flower. Third, there is also a story that the bachelor put a bachelor button flower in his lapel when he decided to go courting.

Once a common crop weed, cornflowers are now considered at risk of extinction in northern Europe. They have escaped from cultivation in places, but wild cornflowers have become exceedingly rare. The explanation seems to be changes in agriculture. Mechanical seeding and harvesting replaced hand seeding and harvesting, and the seeds were better screened to exclude weed seeds. But probably more important was the use of herbicides on the fields after the Second World War.

In southern Europe wild cornflowers are not considered endangered, and of course millions are planted as garden flowers every year, all over the world.

And yet, from a common weed to a rare species in about 100 years...!

It makes you stop to think about how many ways daily life has changed in that century--mechanized agriculture, supermarkets and international trade in food, plastics of all sorts, electricity, freezers, and microwave ovens--to name a few that would affect the life and times of a crop weed.

References:
Durant, M. *Who Named the Daisy? Who Named the Rose? A Roving Dictionary of North American Wild Flowers.* St. Martin's Press, New York. 1983.
Eland, S. C. *Plant Biographies* 2013.
Martin, L. C. *Garden Flower Folklore.* The Globe Pequot Press, Chester CN 1987
PDR (Physician's Desk Reference) for Herbal Medicine. 4th edition. Thompson Healthcare, Montvale, NJ. 2007.

Plant Story – Beautiful Blanket Flower, Gaillardia

BLANKETFLOWER, *Gaillardia*, is a native you probably know as a garden flower. Native garden flowers are not all that common.

Recently, talking and writing about garden flowers, I looked at the origins of common garden flowers and noticed that only a few of them are native to central North America. The simplest explanation is time. Europeans first encountered these American plants in the early 1800s, so that's the earliest that they might have been considered for European-style flower gardens. In contrast, many European and Asian plants have been grown in gardens for 2,000 years. The consequences of long periods in cultivation include familiarity--how often do we favor the plants we grew up with? In addition, cultivation changes plants to make them more attractive in gardens, creating multiple colors, multiple sizes (for example, dwarf varieties), doubled flowers, high and predictable seed germination, good survival of transplanted cuttings. It reduces undesirable characteristics such as spines and aggressive spreading. Roses, lilies, most iris, crocuses, peonies, dahlias, daffodils and narcissus, tulips, and lilacs--to name a few--are all from Eurasia.

Blanket flowers are North American natives—unusual for a garden flower.

American plants have lots of garden potential, and many are available from seed companies and nurseries. A few plants from central North America have, in fewer than 300 years, become garden stars. One is the blanket flower, *Gaillardia*.

Wild blanket flowers are found all across North America: there are twelve species, some with very limited ranges.

A thirteenth blanket flower is the garden blanket flower, *Gaillardia x grandiflora*. Garden blanket flower is a hybrid of the two widespread species, *G. aristiata* (blanketflower) of the west and northwest and *G. pulchella* (Indian blanket or firewheel) of south and southeastern North America. Interspecific hybrids allow gardeners to combine the good characteristics of two species, but often they are infertile. The genes of the two plants work well enough to make a live hybrid, but when they start to divide and recombine in reproduction, problems develop because the chromosomes from the two different species don't exactly match.

When breeders are lucky or wait long enough, a seed might form in which instead of one copy of each parent's chromosomes, it has two. That plant will likely be fertile, because it has two copies of each chromosome which pair nicely. The new hybrid has twice the chromosomes of either parent but that is rarely a problem to plants. ((Terminology: If the parents were diploid (with two copies), the new hybrid is tetraploid (tetra for four)). To breeders, it is a boon, because the four copies of the chromosomes take up more space than two copies, so a bigger nucleus is required and a bigger cell. Building the same shaped plant, bigger cells form bigger plants, so tetraploid hybrids often have bigger flowers than their diploid ancestors. Plant breeders love big flowers because gardeners love big flowers.

I should add that to make bigger cells takes more material, so tetraploid hybrids often grow more slowly and require more water and nutrients than diploids, but rarely dramatically more.

Thus, you can find wild blanket flower in native grasslands and meadows all over North America and buy wild forms for your garden. But also, all across the world, you can buy *Gaillardia x grandiflora* for the garden. Garden blanketflower comes in a variety of patterns and colors. It is a short lived perennial and will reseed itself, at least for a few years.

It is a story of domestication, showing one pathway for developing garden plants native to central North America.

Iris, All the Colors of the Rainbow

IRIS IS A COMMON GARDEN PLANT all around the world.

The genus *Iris*, in the iris family, Iridaceae, has about 280 species, distributed all around the Northern Hemisphere, from Alaska eastward to Japan. People have been attracted to irises for a very long time--Pharaoh Thutmose III had irises that he brought back from his conquest of Syria (1479 BC) painted on his tomb.

> According to the legend, iris plants grew where Iris, goddess of the rainbow, walked.

The name iris is from the Greeks. Iris was the goddess of the rainbow in Greek mythology. It was her job to take the souls of dead women to the Elysian Fields. She further brought messages from the gods to people on earth, traveling down the rainbow. Juno, queen of the gods, was impressed by Iris' diligence and virtue (not the least because Iris repulsed Jupiter's advances) and created the iris plant to reflect the goddess on earth. People in their daily routine would see irises and think of the goddess of the rainbow. Juno created iris plants in all the colors of the rainbow. Wherever Iris walked on earth, iris flowers sprang up.

Most plant groups have flowers in several but not all the colors. Iris are unusual in really having red, orange, yellow, blue and purple flowers. A few are even green or nearly so. The problem with green is that a flower is advertising for pollinators such as bees or butterflies to come to it. Green flowers against green leaves are not very conspicuous. If people want green flowers, usually plant breeders can eliminate other colors, leaving green. Irises also occur in white, black, brown and multiple colors, going beyond the rainbow.

European irises, *Iris x germanica, Iris x florentina* and *Iris pallida* (the x means the experts think these are not naturally-occurring species but hybrids), the German and Florentine irises, were used medicinally in classical and medieval Europe. In the 1200s, Dominicans in Florence promoted the use of dried iris rhizomes, called orris root.

(Rhizomes are below ground stems and orris root is made from rhizomes, so "root" is technically incorrect. Plants have three organs, roots, stems and leaves, and the structure of an underground stem is different from that of a root). Dried rhizomes of European iris had been used earlier, but this was the beginning of the current tradition. Orris root is produced by drying iris rhizomes for at least a year. During that time chemical changes inside the rhizome create new compounds that not only smell nice, but more important, enhance the smell or taste of things with which powdered orris root is blended. Thus, orris root has been added to potpourri and sachets, wine, beer and gin and a variety of cosmetics. There remains a small orris root industry.

Elsewhere in the world, often irises are more toxic. *Iris versicolor*, the blue flag of the eastern U.S., was considered poisonous by Native Americans and used, if needed, as a purgative and cathartic (meaning, it opens the bowels). *Iris missouriensis*, the Rocky Mountain iris, was used as an emetic (to induce vomiting) by people from the Zuni in the southwest to the Klamath in the northwest, as well as being applied externally for various ailments.

Be sure to enjoy all of the different colors of iris!

References:
Moerman, D.E. 1998. *Native American Ethnobotany*. Timber Press, Portland OR.
Pallida Dalmatica and Orris Root —in Italy, Perfume, Martinis, and Your Garden www.tinyurl.com/z9b9rtm
Stewart, A. 2013 *The Drunken Botanist*. Algonquin Books, Chapel Hill, NC.
Orris-root producers: www.sagrona.com/irises

Eastern Pasqueflower, Anemone patens, Heralding Spring

IT IS APRIL AND THE PASQUEFLOWERS are open! The native plants agree that it is spring.

When I tell people pasqueflower is the first wildflower of spring, they look at me doubtfully because often crocuses and daffodils are in full bloom. But across most of its range, there are no native herbs that flower earlier in the spring than pasqueflower.

Pasqueflower is an anemone, *Anemone patens*. The name refers to its blooming time, from the Old French for Easter. In some places it is called May Day flower--same idea!

Pasqueflowers are the state flower of South Dakota and the provincial flower of Manitoba.

"May Day!" you exclaim, "spring is well under way by then." For you, maybe. But pasqueflower is the state flower of South Dakota, USDA Zone 3 to 5, where the last killing frost is often late in May, and the provincial flower of Manitoba, which has an even shorter growing season.

Although it isn't native east of Michigan and Illinois, *Anemone patens* is called the eastern pasqueflower because the one other pasqueflower in North America is found on the Pacific Coast.

Many sources call eastern pasqueflower *Pulsatilla patens*, not *Anemone patens*. Right now the correct name has not been agreed upon by the botanical community. Pasqueflowers are clearly special anemones. They are found all over the world. For example, *Pulsatilla/Anemone chinensis* is an important Chinese medicinal herb (*bái tóu wēng*, translated "hoary-headed geezer," a name that reflects the distinctive seed heads of pasqueflowers).

However, in the *Flora of North America*, Vol. 3, published in 1997, a team of experts looked at the characteristics of pasqueflowers, compared them with anemones and hepaticas and decided the differences were trivial. All the species of pasqueflower, anemone and hepatica should be in the same genus, they concluded. The name *Anemone* had precedence, so all became *Anemone*.

Except, publishing a change doesn't mean all botanists see it that way. When a revision is published, the botanical community considers it and if they are convinced, they apply the changed names, and if not, they ignore the changes. So, currently some botanists are using the name *Anemone* for the pasqueflowers and some are sticking to *Pulsatilla*.

Where does that leave us users of scientific names? In limbo. The easy approach is to pick an expert (current reference) and use whatever name they use. Or you can go with your personal opinion. I'll follow the *Flora of North America's* decisions so I'm using *Anemone*.

One practical consequence of this situation: When searching the web or an index for pasqueflowers, try both *Anemone* and *Pulsatilla*.

By either scientific name, pasqueflower is in the buttercup family, Ranunculaceae. Buttercups are characteristically early spring wildflowers, found in cool north temperate regions (northern Europe, Siberia, northern North America) and toxic or at least not edible. All of those fit anemones including the pasqueflowers as well as buttercups generally.

The fresh foliage can irritate the skin, sometimes to the point of blisters. The Blackfeet used a poultice of pasqueflower leaves as a counter irritant and the Omaha applied the leaves as a treatment of rheumatism. Blackfeet also enjoyed the practical joke of handing someone pasqueflower leaves as toilet paper.

An old common name for pasqueflower is hartshorn plant. Ground hart (red deer)'s horn releases ammonia and was used to revive people who had fainted by irritating the nose and lungs. The volatile chemicals from pasqueflower leaves have the same effect.

The Dakota Sioux thought every species had its own song. Because it is the first native wildflower in bloom, the pasqueflower's song calls the other plants from the ground. Here is a Dakota song of the pasqueflower (Twin-flower is a translation of their name for pasqueflower):

"The Song of the Twin-Flower

"I wish to encourage the children
Of other flower nations now appearing
All over the face of the earth;
So while they awake from sleeping
And come up from the heart of the earth
I am standing here old and gray-headed."

"When an old Dakota first finds one of these flowers in the springtime, it reminds him of his childhood, when he wandered over the prairie hills at play, as free from care and sorrow as the flowers and the birds. He sits down near the flower on the lap of Mother Earth, takes out his pipe and fills it with tobacco. Then he reverently holds the pipe toward the earth, then toward the sky then toward the north, the east, the south and the west. After this act of silent invocation he smokes. While he smokes he meditates upon all the changing scenes of his lifetime, his joys and sorrows, his hopes, his accomplishments, his disappointments and the guidance which unseen powers have given him in bringing him thus far on the way and he is encouraged that he will be guided to the end. After finishing his pipe he rises and plucks the flower and carries it home to show his grandchildren, singing as he goes The Song of the Twin-Flower, which he learned as a child and which he now in turn teaches his grandchildren. "

(song translated by A. McG. Beede, that and quote from Gilmore pp 80-82)

It is difficult to find what I call Native American plant folklore--stories about plants that are unrelated to their practical uses. This quote approaches that, giving us the Dakota tradition that recognizes the pasqueflower as leading the plants, both into flower and into seed. If you see pasqueflowers this year, I hope you will stop for a moment to review your life and your blessings and to share the story with those with you.

References:
Farrar, J. 1990. *Field Guide to the Wildflowers of Nebraska and the Great Plains.* Nebraska Game and Parks Commisssion, Lincoln NE .
Gilmore, M. R. 1919. *Uses of Plants by the Indians of the Missouri River Region.* University of Nebraska Press, Lincoln NE. www.tinyurl.com/gtty3fw
Kindscher, K. 1992. *Medicinal Wild Plants of the Prairie.* University of Kansas Press, Lawrence, KS.
Moerman, D.E. 1998. *Native American Ethnobotany.* Timber Press, Portland OR.
Pulsatilla vulgaris - www.tinyurl.com/h589f7x

Orange, Oranges and Carrots

DO YOU REMEMBER the James Burke tv series Connections showing surprising relationships between unrelated things? There are plant stories like that, for example, of orange, carrots and politics.

Wild carrots, *Daucus carota*, known as Queen Ann's lace in the U.S. (parsley family, Apiaceae) are native all across Europe and the Middle East. Humans have used carrots medicinally for a very long time. Carrots were first domesticated in Afghanistan, producing a readily-grown carrot that was, however, stringy and bitter. These carrots, distributed from Afghanistan, were multicolored: purple, red, orange, yellow and off-white, but especially purple and whitish. People all over Eurasia grew them for medicine, but also as a food flavoring. Like bay leaves or cloves of garlic, they were added for flavor but not necessarily eaten.

Eating carrots was once a political act.

About 1600, plant breeders in Holland bred a truly edible carrot. Everyone agrees that all our modern carrot varieties, even the heritage carrots, are derived from carrot varieties created in Holland at the beginning of the 17th century.

These carrots were orange.

Nobody can prove that the Dutch growers had a political agenda creating an orange carrot, but, whether or not they did, soon after that the orange carrot became very political.

The connection is this:

The provinces of the Netherlands became part of Spain when Mary, Duchess of Burgundy, whose lands included the Netherlands, married the Holy Roman Emperor Archduke Maximillian of Austria in 1477. Their son Philip married Joanna, daughter of Ferdinand of Aragon and Isabella of

Castile. Philip and Joanna's son Charles was King of Castile and Aragon as well as Holy Roman Emperor and Duke of Burgundy.

Meanwhile, in the early 1500's Protestantism swept through the Netherlands and many people embraced the new religion. The kings in Spain, (Charles V (1500-1558), Philip II (1527-1598), Philip III (1578-1621) and Philip IV (1605-1665)) remained Catholic, militantly so, and treated Protestants as heretics. Recant or die!

Spanish rule of the Netherlands became increasingly repressive. Spain's governor of two of the provinces of the Netherlands, Zeeland and Utrecht, William, Prince of Orange (1553-1584), supported his subjects until, when the Dutch resistance turned to rebellion in the late 1560s, he became their leader.

Orange became the color of the Protestants. This was a coincidence.

The city and province of Orange (also spelled Oranje), where William was prince, had nothing to do with the color orange. In what is now France, Orange is north of Avignon. Its name goes back to Roman times, as Arausio, unrelated to oranges or the color orange. There was no orange in Prince William's heraldry, either.

However, in that same century, oranges and the word orange came to Northern Europe.

Citrus fruits, including oranges, are native to the Far East. They gradually spread to India and the Middle East. By that time, Islamic empires ranged from Bagdad to Cairo to

Seville and trade with Christian Europe was very limited. Oranges were brought to Europe by the Moors and grown in the little band of southern Spain that is warm enough to raise oranges. For the most part political divisions kept them in Spain.

In 1492 Ferdinand of Aragon and Isabella of Castile succeeded in defeating the last Moorish kingdom on the Iberian Peninsula. That put all Spain's orange groves in Christian hands as well. The monarchs and their descendants turned their attention to Europe. Spanish orange producers began selling their oranges across northern Europe, facilitated by the fact that the King of Aragon and Castile was also the Holy Roman Emperor and Duke of Burgundy. Tasty sweet oranges (*Citrus sinensis*, lemon family Rutaceae) were brought to Europe about that time. Arriving in northern Europe in the late 1400s and especially the 1500s, oranges were a hit. Since the fruit was new, it had no name in English, Dutch, German or..., so generally the name was based on the Castilian *naranja* or Portuguese *laranja* from the Arabic *naranj*. That came out "orange" in English, "*oranje*" in Dutch.

At the time, European languages did not distinguish the color orange with its own word. It was "reddish yellow" or "yellowish red". Within a few years of the adoption of the word for the fruit, the same word was being used as a color name. (1557 for the first use of orange as a color word in English).

Thus, when, in the 1570s, Prince William of Orange rallied the Protestant Dutch rebels, people hearing it thought of oranges and the color orange.

(That is why Dutch settlers in South Africa called their country the Orange Free State and the flag of Ireland has an orange band.)

Whether or not the Dutch growers were making a point by creating a better ORANGE carrot (seems likely to me), the carrot got caught up in the politics of the 1600s. One of the few orange foods, Protestants embraced carrots, growing them in large numbers. At the same time, traditional Catholics rejected them. For at least a century, eating orange carrots was a political statement!

The fight for Dutch independence was protracted: Spain did not recognize Dutch independence until 1648. The family of William, Prince of Orange, has led Holland since his time.

Modern carrots have been bred in a rainbow of colors, by crossing wilder carrots with the tasty domestic carrots and selecting for the edible characteristics of the orange parent and the colors of the purple or red or yellow or white parent.

And we have long forgotten the politics of orange carrots. But in the 1600s, a new color, a revolutionary leader and a new vegetable converged to make eating carrots a political act.

References:
The Carrot Museum www.carrotmuseum.co.uk All your carrot questions answered!
Grieve, Mrs. M. 1931. *A Modern Herbal.* www.tinyurl.com/857z5rx
McPhee, J. 2000. *Oranges.* Farrar, Stauss and Giroux, New York.
Roose, M. L., R. K. Soost and J. W. Cameron. 1995. Citrus (Rutaceae). pp. 443-449 IN: J. Smartt and N. W. Simmonds, *Evolution of Crop Plants.* 2nd ed. Longman, London.
Vaughan, J. G. and G. Geissler. 1997. *The New Oxford Book of Food Plants.* Oxford, Oxford University Press.
Webber, H. J., revised by W. Reuther and H. W. Lawton. 1967-1989. *History and Development of the Citrus Industry.* The Citrus Industry, revised edition. www.tinyurl.com/jnkyw5p

American Squashes

SORTING OUT THE SQUASHES is a job for experts, which I am not. They are wonderfully confused.

"True squashes" are plants in the genus *Cucurbita* (Cucurbitaceae, cucumber family). About 15 species make up *Cucurbita*, all of them native to the Americas. Melons, such as cantalope in the genus *Cucumis,* watermelon, in the genus *Citrullus* and others--all the melons--are from Asia, Africa or Europe.

None of the squashes are able to survive more than a touch of frost and so all came from warm regions of southern North America, Central America and northern South America. Ten of the species of squash are wild species and five were long ago domesticated. All were originally vines (a few crop varieties are bushes) generally with golden flowers. All are monoecious, meaning they have two quite distinct types of flower on each plant, in fact on each branch, one flower that only produces pollen ("male") and another that does not produce any pollen but contains the ovary and develops fruits with the seeds inside ("female"). In their native range, there are bees which specialize in pollinating the squashes (*Peponapis* and *Xenoglossa,* squash bees), but honey bees and other small bees are effective pollinators as well.

Squashes were probably domesticated for their seeds.

Generally we call squashes vegetables, but from the plant's point of view they are fruits since they contain the seeds. Vegetable is a word that refers to the plant's use in human life, not the plant's own characteristics. The word fruit, for botanists, refers to the function in the plant's life, that is, as a container for seeds.

Five squash species were domesticated: *Cucurbita argyrosperma* (formerly C. *mixta*), C. *ficifolia*, C. *maxima*, C. *moschata* and C. *pepo*. Domestication probably began the confusion that pervades modern squashes. The records look something like this: *Cucurbita pepo* is one of the longest-domesticated plants known: it was grown by people in southern Mexico 10,000 years ago. *Cucurbita moschata* was domesticated, also in southern Mexico, at least 6,900 years ago. The earliest find of *Cucurbita argyrosperma* grown in human settlements was in southern Mexico about 5,000 years ago and C. *ficifolia* is recorded from villages in coastal Peru about the same time, 5,000 years ago. The last domesticated squash, C. *maxima*, was grown by people in coastal Peru 4,000 years ago (2,000 BC). Those are the oldest records known for each species in cultivation, so actual domestication could be substantially longer ago.

The squashes were probably first cultivated for their seeds. The seeds of wild forms are edible, but the flesh of wild squash fruits is quite bitter. Domestication is the process in which a plant, by being planted, tended and harvested by people, develops characters that adapt it to being cultivated, such as easily-gathered seeds, and characters that people like, such as non-spiny stems and large fruit.

After domestication, the peoples of the Americas traded squashes, spreading them all over and developing varieties. Some squash species were certainly domesticated more than once, so the oldest record is only part of the story. By the time of European contact, people as far north as New England grew squashes, many people grew several different squashes, and there were diverse varieties, some grown for seeds and others grown to be eaten cooked and others that could be eaten raw.

You will have noted that although I usually use exact common names, I've been talking in terms of scientific names (or generalizing). That's because the common names don't match the scientific names in squashes. That is highly unusual among plants, but it is the situation for squashes.

It was probably a confused mix of squash varieties before European contact, but Europeans added to the confusion. Europeans encountered squashes everywhere they landed—New England, Virginia, Cuba, Mexico, Brazil, Peru. They took the seeds back to Europe--or to India, or Japan, or wherever they were sailing. As any zucchini grower knows, squashes often produce exuberantly. Beginning with a diverse group of squashes, Europeans carried them all over the world, where new groups of people grew them and selected shapes and colors they liked. The basic squash species do not cross, even when grown in the same garden, so we don't have a hybrid swarm. What we have instead is an array of similar vegetables produced from different, related plant species. Merchants and shoppers gave similar vegetables the same name, naturally unconcerned about what species the squash was. As a result, the names of the vegetables don't match the scientific names, an unusual situation.

The basic distinction in squashes is summer squashes and winter squashes. And the difference between them is that summer squashes are immature fruits, harvested while the rind is soft and the seeds immature. Winter squashes are mature squash fruits. Summer squash, being soft, must be eaten quickly. In contrast the hard rinds of winter squashes protect them so that they can be stored for some time, that is, into the winter. In addition to hard rinds, winter squashes have mature, viable seeds. Most summer squashes are botanically *C. pepo* but some are *C. ficifolia*. Summer squashes include cocozelle squash, cousa squash, crooknecks, patty pan (scallop), trombonchino (zucchetta), yellow squash and zucchini. Summer squashes are called vegetable marrows in British English. Winter squashes can be *C. argyrosperma*, *C. maxima*, *C. moschata* and *C. pepo* botanically and include vegetables called acorn squash, amber squash, autumn cup, banana squash, buttercup squash, butternut, carnival, delicata, hubbard, spaghetti, sweet dumpling squash and turban squash.

Pumpkins are ripe squash fruits, so they could be included in winter squashes. Pumpkins can be any of the four species, C. *argyrosperma*, C. *maxima*, C. *moschata* and C. *pepo*. I'll write about pumpkins another time.

Experts can tell you which species the squash is, using seed color, stem characteristics and other clues. Like most consumers, I don't really care if the winter squash is *Cucurbita maxima* or C. *moschata*, but it is unusual, even in the complexity of domesticated crops, that the species and vegetable names are so mixed up. With most crops, the common name points to one scientific name and vice versa (watermelon is *Citrullus lanatus,* the pea is *Pisum sativum*). I stated above that any of four species can be winter squash. The reverse is true, for example *Cucurbita pepo* varieties are summer squashes, winter squashes and pumpkins. All mixed up!

The term squash itself is interesting. The *Oxford English Dictionary* gives the origin as from the Narragansett word *asquutasquash* < *asq* raw, uncooked. The "-ash" is a plural ending.

The Narragansetts lived (and live) in Rhode Island. They encountered European settlers starting about 1620. The first report of the word squash for the cucurbit fruit is from 1643 in Roger Williams' *A Key into the Language of America,* a Narragansett grammar and dictionary. Williams wrote "*askútasquash,* their Vine apples, which the English from them call Squashes, about the bignesse of Apples of several colours, a sweet light wholesome refreshing." His next entry is " Uppakumíneash - the seed of them. " Note that because this is an American plant, there was no English word for it.

F. B. O'Brien in the online Algonquin dictionary (Narragansett is an Algonquin-group language) wrote that the literal meaning of *askútasquash* was "raw plant that can be eaten". He wrote "The English word "squash" is derived from this Narragansett. The English took the part "squash" (which they did not realize was already plural!) and added "es" to make the new word "squashes". Other Narragansett words that may be of interest are: *askootasquash* ("cucumbers", an English import) and *quonooasquash* ("gourds") and *monaskootasquash* ("melons"). All have the root -ask or -asq meaning "green, raw, natural". The word *asquash* was used in general to mean "edible things green and raw". " (For the record, melons were new to the Narragansett too. There are no melons native to the New World.)

I imagine:
    Englishman "What is that?"
    Narragansett: "Those are askútasquash."
    Englishman "Oh, squashes!"
    Narragansett sighs at the mangling of his language.

Curiously, English already had a word squash, which you can find in Shakespeare in Twelfth Night (1623 i. v. 152)" Asa squash is before tis a pescod" and *Winter's Tale* (1623 i. ii. 162) "This Kernell, This squash, this Gentleman.." Here, a squash is the unripe pod of a pea and when applied to a person in *Winter's Tale,* contemptuous. The verb, "to squash (crush flat)" comes from Old French *esquasser* and is related to the verb quash. The noun meaning pea pod used by Shakespeare is believed to have been derived from the verb squash.

Not only are squashes American, but their name is from a native American word. There are a lot of convergent words in modern English, where two words from different origins come to be spelled and said the same. Squash and squash are obviously two (one?) of them.

Europeans spread squashes from the Americas all over the world, leading to the diverse and curious varieties found in Asia, India and Italy in addition to all the diversity in the Americas. It is possible but not easy to identify the species of a squash--I recommend just enjoying squashes!

References:
O'Brien, F. B. *Algonquin Language Revival* Chapter 7: Corn, Fruits, Berries and Trees, www.tinyurl.com/hmx6k6m
Simpson, B.B. and M. Orgazaly. 2014 *Plants in Our World.* 2nd ed. McGraw-Hill, New York.
Smartt, J. and N. W. Simmonds. 1995. *Evolution of Crop Plants*. 2nd ed. Longman, London.
Squash http://whatscookingamerica.net/squash.htm
"squash" The *Oxford English Dictionary* online
van Wyck, B-E. 2005. *Food Plants of the World*. Timber Press, Portland OR.
Williams, R., 1643, *A Key to the Language of America*, Gregory Dexter publisher, London (p 103)
www.tinyurl.com/j7xpvvc

Colorful Columbines, Aquilegia

EVERYBODY KNOWS COLUMBINE, right?

Columbines, *Aquilegia* species, are distinctive plants related to anemones and buttercups (in the buttercup family, Ranunculaceae).

Actually, where you live makes a big difference to what you think a columbine looks like. In eastern North America, there is only one native columbine, *Aquilegia canadensis*. It has red sepals and spurs on the outside with yellow petals, stigmas and stamens inside.

Hummingbirds like red columbines; bumble bees like blue ones.

The situation in Europe is similar. There is one common columbine, *Aquilegia vulgaris*. However, it has blue to purple sepals with white petals, stigma and stamens. There are 21 columbine species in the mountains of Europe, of which *A. vulgaris* is by far the most widespread. In Latin, "vulgaris" means common, so the common European columbine is aptly named. But whichever columbine you see in Europe, it is likely to be blue or purple with white petals, stigma and stamens.

If you live in either of those areas, you are likely to have a particular image of columbine in your mind. It is just that those two images are different!

In North America, as soon as you reach the Rocky Mountains going west, there stops being just one columbine. *The Flora of North America* lists 21 species in North America, so there are 20 species of columbine in the western North America! They are yellow, blue, white, red, pink…a rainbow of colors.

Another 20 or more species are spread across Asia, some with large ranges, many with very small ranges. Columbines are a Northern Hemisphere group of cooler climates and higher elevations. I'll talk about North America, since I don't know as much about Eurasian columbines.

The blue to purple Rocky Mountain columbine *Aquilegia coerulea*, is the state flower of Colorado. (You will see the scientific name as *A. caerulea* but the three most authoritative sources I could find spell it *A. coerulea*.)

Of course, cultivated columbines come in many colors. On top of wild species with distinct colors, columbine species readily hybridize. The colors of the hybrids add even more available colors.

Columbines cross between species when planted together in gardens, but they also do it in the wild, in the places where one species encounters another. So when you are hiking in western North America, you can encounter columbines that don't fit anything in your pocket field guide, because you are looking at a hybrid population.

This color variation has attracted North American botanists for easily 100 years. Numerous research projects have looked at why columbines hybridize and what happens to the hybrids.

The answer begins with the benefits of the different colors. The flowers of each species are adapted to attract particular pollinators. The distinctive spurs hold nectar (sugar water). Hummingbirds, hawk moths and bumblebees are the most common pollinators of columbines in North America. Hummingbirds are strongly attracted to red. Hawk moths are often nocturnal. At night, light colors are more visible. Bumblebees generally prefer blue, purple and yellow columbines.

The different pollinators also prefer different flower-shapes. Hummingbird-pollinated columbines tend to be nodding with narrow flowers, because hummingbirds easily hover below the flower when taking nectar. In comparison, bumblee-pollinated columbines have sturdy, upward-facing flowers so that the bumblebee can land when visiting.

Hawk moth-pollinated columbines often have long narrow flowers, which extend out beyond the leaves rather than sag downward.

Thirdly, hummingbirds' tongues can reach into the columbine's spurs, but the spurs have to be rather broad and not too long. Some species of hawkmoth have very long tongues and can reach into deep, narrow, curved spurs for nectar. Bumblebees like nectar but the spur has to be short and broad. Spurless columbines--and there are varieties and species with spurs so short they are hard to recognize as columbine flowers--are generally pollinated by bees.

Hybrids are created when a pollinator carries pollen from the flower of one species to another species. Hummingbirds, hawk moths and bumblebees will all occasionally check out flowers that are not their preferred color and shape, and those visits can cause hybridization between species. The hybrid is usually less attractive to the pollinators of both its parent species.

Habitat matters too. Different columbine species usually have different habitats. For example, some grow in deep shade, others on open rocky slopes. The hybrid doesn't fit any real environment well and while it may survive, because it is growing poorly, it will flower less and mature fewer seeds, likely slowly dying out.

Consequently, despite the ease of hybridization of columbines, the preferences of different pollinators for different flower characteristics and their environmental requirements keep columbine species distinct and separate.

Take some time to watch hummingbirds or hawk moths or bumblebees visiting columbines. Great entertainment!

Columbines come in many different colors and cross easily between species. Explaining the origin of all the variation and why they stay different in nature continues to keep biologists busy. Flor and coauthors, publishing a large and complex paper in 2012, don't imply they've answered all the questions but rather call further study of columbines an "exciting opportunity." If you aren't in need of a research project right now, just enjoy the diversity of columbines.

References:
(and there are many other studies, especially of North American columbines)
Bastida, J.M., J. M. Alcántara, P.J. Rey, P. Vargas, C. M. Herrera. 2010. Extended phylogeny of *Aquilegia:* the biogeographical and ecological patterns of two simultaneous but contrasting radiations. *Plant Systematics and Evolution.* 284:171-185.
Brunet, J., Z. Larson-Rabin and C. M. Stewart. 2012. The distribution of genetic diversity within and among populations of the Rocky Mountain columbine: the impact of gene flow, pollinators, and mating system. *International Journal of Plant Sciences* 173(5): 484-494.
Chase, V. C. and P. H. Raven. 1975. Evolutionary and ecological relationships between *Aquilegia formosa* and *A. pubescens* (Ranunculaceae), two perennial plants. *Evolution.* 29 (3): 474-486.
Flor, S., M. Li, B. Oxelman, R. Viola, S. A. Hodges, L. Ometto and C. Varotto. 2012. Spatiotemporal reconstruction of the *Aquilegia* rapid radiation through next-generation sequencing of rapidly evolving cpDNA regions. *New Phytologist.* 298: 579-592.
Grant, V. 1952. Isolation and hybridization between *Aquilegia formosa* and *A. pubescens.* El *Aliso.* 2 (4): 341-360.
Grant, V. and E. J. Temeles. 1992. Foraging ability of rufous hummingbirds on hummingbird flowers and hawkmoth flowers. *Proceedings of the National Academy of Sciences,* U.S.A. 89: 9400-9404.
Wittmore, A.T. 21. Aquilegia Linnaeus, Sp. Pl. 1: 533. 1753; Gen. Pl. ed. 5, 237, 1754. In *Flora of North America* www.tinyurl.com/zznxvt6

Reasons to Like Primroses, Primula

I'VE BEEN TRYING FOR YEARS to grow primroses, genus *Primula*. Last year I stuck three sad little plants, rescued from the nursery's end-of-the-season sale, into my yard and ooh, this spring all three are alive and flowering!

What is special about primroses?

They are pretty!

Also, I associate them with the literature set in England I read as a child. Primroses grew in the well-tended gardens of the ladies in quaint English villages.

The primrose path was not a respectable garden lane.

In addition, primroses were the usual example of a curious plant reproductive system, studied by Charles Darwin himself and carefully described to us by my professor at Berkeley, Herbert Baker, an Englishman with a fondness for them.

One of the first things I had to do as a botany student was to figure out that the primrose was not a rose, with which I was familiar, nor an evening primrose, with which I was also familiar. Today I can recognize a primrose, but that's recent. For a long time I knew primroses by what they were not.

Primroses are in the genus *Primula*, family Primulaceae. There are nine genera in the primrose family, distributed all over the world, but especially in the Northern Hemisphere. The only one I recognize, even today after 40 years studying plants, is *Dodecatheon*, shooting star.

The USDA plants website lists 20 *Primula* species, genuine primroses, in North America, all native except two--and yet almost none of them grow in the places I've lived, New York, Ohio, Michigan, Nebraska and California. Four species do grow somewhere in Colorado, but I have not yet seen them in nature.

Roses and evening primroses, both NO relation to primroses, are much more familiar to me.

Why try to grow an unfamiliar plant?

Well, because of primrose's happy reputation.

Primroses bloom early in the spring. The name, *Primula*, is from the Latin word for first, *primus*, referring to their early spring flowering. For England, they are one of the flowers that symbolize the coming of spring. (In England the common primroses are often called cowslips.)

The Primrose Path sticks in my mind as a positive association, but in fact it is from Shakespeare and slightly sinister:

> Doe not as some vngracious pastors doe,
> Showe me the step and thorny way to heauen
> Whiles a puft, and reckles libertine
> Himselfe the primrose path of dalience treads.
> (*Hamlet*, I iii 50)

Primroses had a definite association with wantonness in English folklore.

Folklore also linked primroses to the success of chickens, so that in most places it was bad luck to pick primroses and bring them into the house in the early spring as the hens were starting to lay eggs. In particular the number of primroses picked was the number of fertile eggs the chickens would lay, so bringing in 13 or more primroses was great, but picking only one or two meant there would not be enough eggs this spring. At the beginning of spring, when you'd most want to pick the first primroses to celebrate spring, finding more than 13 might be very difficult. Be careful what you start, you might be hiking a long way for a couple more primrose flowers, even when you don't really believe it affects the chickens.

Oops, the folklore isn't so positive
— but they are still pretty.

One last question: What color is primrose?

Primrose should be the color of primroses, right?

Looking it up, I found the color "primrose" is a light yellow. That is the color of wild primroses in England, the color of *Primula vulgaris*, the common primrose. However, red, blue and nearly purple primroses are common today. It is no longer obvious what color "primrose" is. If you buy primroses from the nursery, as I did, very few of the primroses for sale are primrose-colored primroses. Although *Primula vulgaris*, the common primrose is primrose-colored, other primrose species are not.

A Google search for "primrose color" came up with about half yellow and half pink responses. It does seem logical that primROSE should be a pink, even though it isn't.

Language changes. Primroses are not common garden plants in the United States and only some of the ones sold are yellow. Actually, some of those are too intensely yellow to be called primrose.

My guess is that in England and in Europe generally, people would know light yellow primroses and expect that to be the color "primrose" while in the United States, most people will hear "rose" in the name and expect a pink. What of other English-speaking countries? What color is primrose in Australia or India or Canada?

For certain: Don't buy a primrose-colored garment sight unseen!

References:
Martin, Laura C. 1987. *Garden Flower Folklore*. The Globe Pequot Press, Chester Connecticut.
Vickery, Roy. 1995. *Oxford Dictionary of Plant-Lore*. Oxford University Press, Oxford.

Snowdrops, Leading the Spring Flowers

JUST LIKE THERE'S NO WAY to eliminate Monday--in the sense that there will always be a first day of the work week, no matter what we call it--likewise, every place has a first spring flower.

The snowdrop, *Galanthus nivallis*, is one of those.

These diminutive plants grow from bulbs. Native to the mountains of Europe and southwestern Asia, they are grown all over Europe as early spring flowers and have naturalized there and in the eastern United States.

Snowdrops brought so much bad luck florists wouldn't sell them.

Snowdrops have some 20 related species in the genus *Galanthus,* found from Europe into the Middle East. They are classified in the large, diverse amaryllis family (Amaryllidaceae). (Compare onions, also in the Amaryllidaceae, next chapter). Like snowdrops, most species of *Galanthus* flower in very early spring (before the spring equinox) and are quite tolerant of cold and snow.

In the scientific name, *gala* is Greek for "milk," *anthos* for "flower" and *nivalis* means "snowy." Today they are pretty universally called snowdrops in English, but they have older common names including snow-piercers, dingle-dangle, Candlemas bells, Mary's bells or "The Fair Maid of February."

The name snowdrop is usually reported to come from the shape and color of the flowers. However, Wikipedia, quoting a book entirely on snowdrops which I have not read myself, gives the alternate explanation that pearl earrings called snowdrops were very popular in the 16th century and the current common name is from the similarity of the flowers to the jewelry. (Look online for the portrait of Louise de Lorraine, Queen of France in snowdrop earrings).

People were pleased to see snowdrops in flower. In many parts of Europe snowdrops are the very first plant to flower. Generally in flower in England by February first, they were consequently called Candlemas bells and incorporated into the celebration of Candlemas, the Purification of Saint

Mary, on February 2. They were used to decorate the altar and worn by young girls.

Snowdrops are the English floral symbol for January and in at least one Victorian "language of flowers" system they represented hope and consolation.

> The snowdrop, in purest white arraie
> First rears her hedde on Candlemas daie.
> --An Early Calendar of English Flowers in Garden Flower Folklore

> Thou first-born of the year's delight
> Pride of the dewy glade,
> In vernal green, and virgin white
> They vestal robes array'd.
> --Keble in Nature Notes of an Edwardian Lady

Despite all this positive symbolism, country folk in England frequently considered snowdrops ill-omened. Picking snowdrops and bringing them into the house meant there would be a death in the immediate family. Mid-20th century florists reportedly refused to sell them because of the bad luck they brought. Perhaps this reputation stems from the fact that they emerge from ground wrapped in white sheaths, as if the plant were a tiny body prepared for burial. Another possibility is that since they often grow in graveyards, they developed a sinister association with death. Other white flowers are associated with death, so bad luck from snowdrops may be part of a general reaction.

My yard had snowdrops when I bought it 10 years ago. They persisted with no help from me and spread when I protected them from being stepped on. Here in northern

Colorado I don't see them as early as Candlemas, but often they are in flower the next week and certainly by the first of March. They do well under my maple tree because there they get full sun in early spring but are shaded from the drying Colorado sun later in the growing season.

The foliage disappears by late spring as the bulbs go dormant. This seems tidy but can be a problem. I would like to divide one of my clumps and move another to what I hope is a better location. For two years now, I haven't been able to find the plants in the fall to move them, despite digging where I'd left a marker. I still want to move them, so I'll mark them more carefully this spring and hope for better luck next fall.

Looking in the *Oxford English Dictionary* at "snowdrop," I found that in addition to the flower, it is a name for a military policeman. Apparently it began with Second World War-era American military policemen who wore distinctive white helmets. That uniform isn't worn any more, but, at least in some places, the name persists. You have to enjoy the British whimsey, nicknaming tough military policemen delicate flowers.

Watch for this year's snowdrops.

References:
Holden, E. 1905. *The Natures Notes of an Edwardian Lady.* Archade Publishing, New York
Martin, L. C. 1987. *Garden Flower Folklore.* The Globe Pequot Press, Chester Connecticut
Wikipedia Snowdrops
www.tinyurl.com/78d6lud Accessed 1/13/16

The Indomitable Onion

IT SEEMS LIKE ONIONS have always been part of our diet.

The common onion, *Allium cepa*, is a bulb related to lilies, in the amaryllis family, Amaryllidaceae. (DNA evidence keeps moving the onions around, from the lily family to their own family and now with amaryllis).

The common onion is not known in the wild. That is, it is only found in gardens or where a garden was very obviously abandoned. Since it must have started as a wild plant, "not found in the wild" might mean the wild forms went extinct or that the cultivated onion is enough changed from its wild ancestors to be considered different, or the cultivated onion is a hybrid that does not occur in nature.

Onions were sacred in ancient Egypt.

If you can't find wild *Allium cepa*, it is hard to know where it is native. Today the common onion is found ALL over the world–170 countries grow it for domestic use–so modern distributions are no help. Archaeology and the patterns of relationship suggest onions are from somewhere in Asia, but there is no consensus as to exactly where.

The story is complicated by the existence of 260-850 species in the genus *Allium*, native all over the Northern Hemisphere. While *Allium cepa* is grown and sold more than any of the other *Allium*, lots of people grow or gather other onion species. Names obscure some of the relationships: a oniony wild plant is often called a wild onion (*Allium textile* is the prairie wild onion of Colorado), but *Allium porrum* are leeks, *Allium sativum* garlic, and *Allium schoenoprasum* chives.

From 5,000 years ago, at minimum, people have grown onions, *Allium cepa*. They are known from archaeological sites going back that far in both Babylon and Egypt.

Eaten, onions provided food and water. Both leaves and bulbs could be eaten. They grew easily in most soils and most climates. The bulbs stored very well, fresh or dried.

In addition, onions have medicinal value. They inhibit bacteria, for example, so putting them on a cut was a wise move. But they also soothed blisters, bruises, and insect stings.

"Those suffering from coughs, asthma and constrictions in the chest should eat boiled onions or onions baked under the embers, served with sugar and a little fresh butter," writes the author of the *Tacunium Sanitatis*, a health manual from medieval Europe.

The complete list of things treated with onions is very long! It includes sore throats, colds and flu; skin inflammations; restoring circulation in frozen feet; reducing lethargy and invigorating a poor appetite; clearing out the head; healing the ear of both pain and noise, to name a few.

Onions had enough obvious medical value that in much of the Old World, they came to be a universal remedy. Some of that comes down to us as advice such as from Cambridgeshire, England: "Eat an onion every day before breakfast and all the doctors might ride on one horse."

From prehistoric times, onions were seen as protective, both by repelling evil (for example keeping away snakes) and also taking it into themselves (using modern terminology, we'd say absorbing germs). Traditional English households kept an onion, cut in half, hanging near the doorway to protect the inhabitants. It is widely repeated that the inhabitants of God's Providence House in Chester escaped the plague because cut onions were laid at the door to the building. *The Oxford Dictionary of Plant-Lore* points out that the last plague outbreak in Chester was in 1648 but that God's Providence House was not built until 1652. Nevertheless, the story bolstered onions' reputation for protecting people.

The ancient uses read as superstition, but modern, controlled experiments have shown onions to be effective in controlling atherosclerosis and countering loss of appetite. Onion juice has definite anti-bacterial action.

Some of the best-documented information on onions in the ancient world is from Egypt. There, onions were important enough that wages and taxes were sometimes paid in onions.

But beyond that, Egyptians wound the onion in a complex of religious and philosophical beliefs. Onions were healing and protective and freshened the breath. That brought them to be heavily used with the dead: to preserve the body, but also to connect to the afterlife and protect the person as they crossed over from this world to the next.

Egyptians saw a symbol (or microcosm) of eternity in the spherical shape and concentric rings of onions.

Cultures from the Hindus to the Egyptians to 17th century Europe considered the onion an aphrodisiac. In ancient Egypt that meant that, revered though onions were, priests could not eat them. In France it led to offering newlywed couples onion soup the morning after their wedding.

I ate onions raw in the garden as a grade-school girl. And yet, I find it hard to visualize the Egyptian workers on the pyramids at their lunch break, eating raw onions as if they were apples. Some of that is a function of the type of onion. I have always worked with yellow onions, but ancient Egypt favored a milder, white onion. To test this I took a big bite out of a red (sweet, Spanish) onion yesterday. Wow! it was sharp! I lasted for one more bite but then I'd had enough. Raw onions eaten like apples aren't for me.

Cooked, onions are quite different from raw, much less sharp-tasting, and in fact, quite sweet.

Consider this 18th century poem of Johnathan Swift's, appropriate today:

> Come, follow me by the smell,
> Here are delicate onions to sell
> I promise to use you well.
> They make the blood warmer,
> You'll feed like a farmer;
> For this is every cook's opinion,
> No savory dish without an onion
> But, lest your kissing should be spoil'd,
> Your onions must be thoroughly boil'd:
> Or else you may spare
> Your mistress a share,
> The secret will never be known:
> She cannot discover
> The breath of her lover,
> But think it as sweet as her own.

Share onions!

References:

Agaravante, M. *The Onion's Role in Ancient Egypt*. San Diego Examiner. Dec. 1, 2013. www.tinyurl.com/h2xw86s Accessed 1/4/16.

Culpeper, N. 1652. *Culpeper's Complete Herbal and The English Physician*. Onion.

Tacunium Sanitatis, published as *The Four Seasons of the House of Cerruti*. 1983. Arnoldo Mondadori Ed. Original Italy 13th C.

Harrison, L. 2011. *A Potted History of Vegetables*. Lyons Press, Guilford, Connecticut.

onions-usa.org Domestic Onion Production. Accessed 1/7/16

Stevens, P. F. (2001 onwards). Angiosperm Phylogeny Website. Version 12, July 2012 [and more or less continuously updated since]." www.tinyurl.com/f746l

Angiosperm Phylogeny website. Amaryllidaceae: Allieae.
Swift, J. 1853. *The Poetical Works of Jonathan Swift.* Onions. Boston: Little, Brown and Company. (Swift lived 1667-1745).
Vickery, R. 1995. *The Oxford Dictionary of Plant-Lore.* Oxford U. Press, Oxford.

Yarrow, Achillea millefolium, an Ancient Healing Herb

YARROW, *Achillea millefolium*, is a familiar wildflower with a confused history. A member of the very large sunflower family, Asteraceae, it is quite closely related to wild and cultivated chamomiles.

Yarrow was named *Achillea millefolium* by Linnaeus in 1753. The genus name is based on the idea that Achilles, Spartan hero and demigod in the *Iliad* of Homer, used yarrow to heal wounds. I wanted to include the exact quote and was surprised by what I found. The *Iliad* never mentions yarrow. The healing passage, paraphrased frequently as "Achilles used yarrow to heal his soldiers" is quoted below and is both quite vague and has the healing done by Patroclus. (Bk XI:804-848 "Patroclus tends Eurypylus' wound". *Iliad* A.S. Kline 2009.)

> The wounded Eurypylus replied:...'help me to my black ship, and cut out the arrow-head, and wash the dark blood from my thigh with warm water, and sprinkle soothing herbs with power to heal on my wound, whose use men say you learned from Achilles, whom the noble Centaur, Cheiron, taught. ...'
>
> ....Patroclus lowered the wounded man to the ground, and cut the sharp arrow-head from his thigh. Next he washed the dark blood from the place with warm water, and rubbing a bitter pain-killing herb between his hands sprinkled it on the flesh to numb the agony. Then the blood began to clot, and ceased to flow.

Alternatively, Achilles was reported to have healed the festering spear wound of King Telephus of Mysia. This appears not in the *Iliad* but in other sources of Greek mythology. However, the spear wound of Telephus was cured by scrapings from the spear that caused the injury, suggested by Odysseus, not Achilles, and no mention was made of yarrow.

Yarrow has been healing people for 50,000 years.

Both these stories appeared in the *Natural History* of Pliny the Elder, written in Latin in the first century AD. In Book XXV, Chapter 19 Pliny the Elder wrote:

> Achilles too, the pupil of Chiron, discovered a plant which heals wounds, and which, as being his discovery, is known as the "achilleos." It was by the aid of this plant, they say, that he cured Telephus. Other authorities, however, assert that he was the first[1] to discover that verdigris[2] is an extremely useful ingredient in plasters; and hence it is that he is sometimes represented in pictures as scraping with his sword the rust from off a spear[3] into the wound of Telephus. Some again, are of opinion that he made use of both remedies.

(From John Bostock translator, *Pliny Online*. The notes, if are curious, say "1 Both stories are equally improbable. 2 See B. xxxiv. c. 45. 3 The weapons in early time, it must be remembered, were made of copper or bronze.")

Pliny is pretty unconvincing that Achilles used yarrow to heal, but as far as I can tell, his is the oldest written version of this traditional story. The Trojan War was 1260-1240 BC. Homer lived in the 8th or 9th century BC, 300 years later. Pliny wrote 800 years after that. The identification of yarrow with Achilles is old and strong, but elusive.

The word *millefolium*, means "thousand leaf" or "thousand leaves", referring to the many leaflets on the finely-divided leaves. The usual English name yarrow is apparently derived from *gearwe*, an Anglo-Saxon name, or from the River Yarrow, Gaelic for rough stream. In other European languages, yarrow is commonly called some variation of milfoil and that was what Linnaeus chose for the species name. Very old sources give various names such as *militaris* and *herba militaris* for yarrow, which are versions of "soldier's herb." In European tradition, yarrow was highly regarded for treating wounds, especially bleeding wounds from iron weapons. Gerard in 1599 wrote "The leaves of Yarrow doe close up wounds, and keep them from inflammation…" You can see how that comes from the Achilles myths. The fine leaflets are in fact effective in slowing bleeding so that the blood will clot. Furthermore yarrow is rich in antibiotic compounds. While there are better choices if you can get to a hospital, it is still recognized as an effective plant for treating a bloody sword or knife cut. 3,200 years later, we agree with Achilles (and Chiron and Patroclus).

All over the world, herbal medicinal traditions have embraced yarrow. It goes back millennia in Ayurvedic and Chinese medicine and was used in Native American medicine throughout North America. Indeed, a Neanderthal skull in Spain, from about 50,000 years ago, had traces of yarrow in his or her teeth. Since yarrow is bitter, the researchers believed the Neanderthals used it as medicine, not food.

And that will pretty well tell you why *Achillea millefolium* can be found all over the world. Traders and colonists who set out to the far corners of the world where they couldn't assume any medical care would be available and didn't know what plants they would find there, took reliable medicines with them. Yarrow seeds traveled in the pouches of traders and settlers to be planted around their dwellings, just in case.

Yarrow is an adaptable little plant, liking rich soils and lots of rain but surviving many other places. There isn't much of the world where yarrow can't be found these days.

Finally, I want to note that modern research has found yarrow to be effective for loss of appetite, mild gastrointestinal complaints and more. Check a responsible medical source.

References:
Applequist, Wendy J. and Daniel E. Moerman. 2011. Yarrow (*Achillea millefolium* L.): A neglected panacea? A review of ethnobotany, bioactivity and biomedical research. *Economic Botany.* 65(2): 209-225.
Blumenthal, Mark, ed. 2000. *Herbal Medicine. Expanded Commission E Monographs.* American Botanical Council, Austin, TX.
Bostock, John translator, Pliny Online http://tinyurl.com/
Chandler, R.F., S. N. Hooper and M.J. Harvey. 1982. Ethnobotany and phytochemistry of yarrow *Achillea millefolium*, Compositae. *Economic Botany.* 36 (2): 203-223. Good table of uses by Native Americans
Gerard, John. 1633. *The Herball or the General History of Plants.* Johnson Publishers, London. Reprinted by Dover Publications, Inc. New York. (1975). (Gerard's first edition, 1599, is online but very difficult to navigate. In my edition, "Yarrow or Nose-bleed" is Chapter 438 on p. 1072-3, after Lousewort & Rattle, and before Valerian).
Greenwald, T. Brendler, and C. Jaenicke, eds. 2007. PDR (*Physicians Desk Reference) for Herbal Medicines.* 4th ed. Thompson Publishers, Montvale, NJ.

Translations of the Iliad online:
Butler, Samuel. 1898 *Iliad* The Literature Network. www.tinyurl.com/j6mb85m
Kline, A. S. 2009. *Poetry in Translation. The Iliad.* www.tinyurl.com/mxo4h4l
Murray, A. T. 1924. *Homer. The Iliad with an English Translation in two volumes.* Cambridge, MA., Harvard

University Press; London, William Heinemann, Ltd. 1924.
www.tinyurl.com/jzyrs4s

Pope, Alexander, translator. *The Iliad*. (1725) ebooks@ Adelaide. www.tinyurl.com/h6oh7ou

Daphne, Attractive and Fragrant

WINTER DAPHNE, also called fragrant daphne, *Daphne odora*, is a flowering shrub from Asia. It is in the plant family, Thymelaeaceae, which, because most of its members are Old World, is not well known to Americans. You could call the Thymelaeaceae the daphne family or the spurge laurel family. Daphnes are planted as garden shrubs.

I think of the flowers as white but it is clear from my photos that the buds are pink and the flowers paler pink. The scent is sweet and heavy: I like it very much. I also like that it flowers in early spring but is still flowering a month later.

Daphne was discovered in China because of its wonderful fragrance.

The leaves on my winter daphne have a white rim, as the photos show. The plants grow to 4' tall but after five years mine are barely 3'. The websites say it is hardy in USDA zones 7-9 but I'm in zone 5! My plants do suffer a lot of leaf-browning in winter--see old leaves in the photo below. The most-protected plant turns green and flowers easily a week ahead of the others. So perhaps they struggle with my climate, but they are doing fine.

Daphnes are found all over the Old World. There are about 100 species. They are named for Daphne, a naiad (a water sprite in female form) who was pursued by the god Apollo. His attention was unwanted so Daphne begged help of the rivergod her father. He turned her into the laurel tree, *Laurus nobilis*, to hide her from Apollo. The laurel (also called the bay tree) is not related to the plant called daphne.

Naming a plant that isn't the laurel "laurel" was apparently an intentional word game by Linnaeus, the Swede who, in the 1750s, set up the scientific name system we are still using. The spurge laurel, now *Daphne laureola*, is and was a well-known shrub, native to Europe and the Middle East. Spurges are generally plants in the spurge or poinsettia family, Euphorbiaceae, so this traditional name, spurge laurel, suggested the plant looked like a laurel and a spurge. Many spurges are poisonous, and so is *Daphne laureola*, the spurge laurel. The widely used common name, spurge laurel, likened the plant to two plants well known to Europeans, even though it is not actually very like either one. Linneaus could not resist perpetuating the problem. Since the naiad Daphne was turned into the laurel, *daphne* in Greek means laurel. In addition, in much of Europe a common name of the spurge laurel was laureola, meaning "small laurel" or "laurel branch". In making the scientific name of the spurge laurel *Daphne laureola*, Linneaus named the spurge laurel "laurel laurel," knowing full well it was not related to the laurel, *Laurus nobilis* (laurel family, Lauraceae). In Europe, where people know laurels, spurges and spurge laurels, people undoubtedly enjoyed the joke. It puzzled me.

Not all daphnes are from Europe. My winter daphne, *Daphne odora*, is from China. It has been cultivated since the Song Dynasty, 960-1279 AD. According to an early Chinese herbal, a monk fell asleep below a cliff on Lu Mountain (*Lu Shan*) in Jiangxi Province. In a dream he smelled a fragrance so strong and memorable that he recalled it clearly when he awoke. He climbed up the mountain to find the source of the odor, finding *Daphne odora*. He called the plant "sleeping scent" (*shuixiang*). which has changed over time to the similar-sounding name lucky scent (*ruixiang*).

Winter daphne has been in cultivation so long wild plants in China are hard to verify but it is believed to be native only to China. It "grows everywhere throughout the southern provinces" wrote S-C. Li in 1578 (p. 144). It was recorded in Japan in 1309. Traditional Chinese medicine used lucky scent/winter daphne as a wash for sore throats and small pox.

The vast majority of websites promoting growing winter daphne as a yard plant say absolutely nothing about safety. But like the spurge laurel, it is poisonous. Spurge laurel references say that although that plant is dangerous, it tastes so acrid animals are unlikely to eat it. Winter daphne is part of the University of California, Davis's veterinary poison garden. U. C. D. suggests winter daphne "is best planted in areas not frequented by children or pets. All parts of the plant are toxic, but the berries are most likely to be attractive to pets or children."

A surprising number of familiar plants are poisonous if ingested. Like those others, if you don't eat winter daphne, it won't bother you. And it has beautiful flowers in spring and a fragrance so wonderful you too might climb a mountain to find it.

References:
Allen, B. M. 1993. *Wildflowers of Southern Spain*. Ediciones Santana, Malaga, Spain.
Daphne. Portland Nursery. www.tinyurl.com/jmyggvk Accessed 4/22/15.
Daphne-Siedeblast. 2011-2015. www.tinyurl.com/hehcbacl
Daphne. Wikipedia. www.tinyurl.com/yl524mt Accessed 4/22/15.
Li, -C. 1973 *Chinese Medicinal Herbs. A Modern Edition of a Classic Sixteenth-Century Manual*. F.P. Smith and G.A. Stewart, translators, Dover Publications, Inc., New York. Original Chinese version 1578.
Toxic plant garden. Univeristy of California Davis toxic plant garden. www.tinyurl.com/ztn4nxs Accessed 4/22/15.
Valder, P. 1999. *Garden Plants of China*. Timber Press, Portland, OR.

Peas, Pescods and Pease
Pisum sativum

THE THREE FACES OF PEAS – fresh peas, dried peas, and edible-pod peas--are different enough that it is hard remembering they are all the same thing, peas, *Pisum sativum* (pea family, Fabaceae).

Mostly, when we say "peas" today, we are thinking of shelling peas (garden peas, English peas) especially ones that have been frozen, since peas freeze really well and the season for fresh peas is short.

But it was because they could be dried and stored that peas were one of the very first plants domesticated in the Middle East.

> Peas were important food crops because they store so well.

Archaeologists found peas in Neolithic Near Eastern and European sites, 8,000 to 9,500 years ago. By 7,600 years ago, the peas found in settlements were domesticated peas--grown rather than gathered. Domesticated peas have smooth seeds, unlike their wild relatives, and so can be recognized at an archaeological site. By the Bronze Age (5,000 years ago) peas were being grown in Switzerland, They were widely cultivated in classical Greece and across the Roman Empire. Looking eastward, peas were grown as a vegetable in China from at least 700 AD.

Peas dry relatively easily, store well and are high in protein and vitamins B and C. In addition they contain no toxins and don't cause allergies. They are also bigger than most other seeds available in ancient Eurasia. With all that going for them, it is no surprise they became a staple food.

The wild pea is an annual vine, climbing with tendrils. During domestication bush forms were produced.

The seeds can be green, brown, white, yellow or blue when dry. Dried peas can be ground into powder to make a flour.

As a common food plant, peas accumulated specific terms and folklore. Pea was only one of the English names given the plant in the 16th century. Thomas Hill in *The Gardeners Labyrinth*, the first English-language gardening book, mainly called them peason, sometimes pease or peas. (Hill's book is wonderful for its unstandardized spelling. Hill spells the same word differently on the same page.) The word "pea" is a late addition to English. Apparently people were bothered by a singular that sounded plural: "You dropped a pease" and created a new singular "pea".

Other old terms used with peas include cosh, pescod and squash. You cosh peas to shell them which takes the peas out of the cosh. Shakespeare refers to a pea pod as pescod and an unripe pea pod as a squash. Both pescod and squash were insults if applied to a person.

Norse mythology described peas as having been a gift of the god Thor that should only be eaten on his name-day (Thursday).

A European folk remedy used peas to be rid of warts. For each wart, you wrapped a pea in paper and buried it, saying "As this pea shall rot away, so my warts shall soon decay."

Surely every school child learned, as I did:

Pease porridge hot;
Pease porridge cold;
Pease porridge in the pot,
Nine days old.

The rhyme goes back to the Middle Ages, and refers to what we would today call pea soup. I remember being puzzled by it, not knowing the word porridge or why it would be nine days old. Another virtue of peas is that a pot of old porridge would still be nutritious and reasonably tasty.

Shelling peas is a common task for anyone who grows peas.

Folklore had it that it was good luck to find nine peas in the first pod shelled. Even later in the day, nine peas in a pod were lucky. If you put the nine-pea pod over your door, the first person to walk in under it will have the same name (or initial in some versions of the story) as your future spouse.

Peas were not eaten fresh until the 17th century according to crop historians. I presume that means "were not grown as a crop intended to be eaten fresh" because anyone who has grown peas has grabbed a few off the vine to eat then and there.

Canning (from the early 1800s) and freezing (from the 1920s and 1930s) greatly increased consumption of peas, especially fresh—as opposed to dried—peas, since before that, fresh peas were only available very briefly in the late spring.

Edible-pod peas, called snow peas or sugar snap peas, are even more recent. Some were grown in the early 17th century but only since 1979 were modern varieties developed and promoted.

Production of peas is the fifth largest of the world's legumes, behind soybeans, common beans, peanuts and chickpeas. In addition to their uses as food, peas are often incorporated in animal fodder.

And of course, peas are available for diverse puns.

Let me wish you:

Peas on earth.

References:
Mabey, R. 1987. *The Gardener's Labyrinth* by Thomas Hill. Oxford University Press, Oxford.

National Geographic.2008. Edible. *An Illustrated Guide to the World's Food Plants*. National Geographic Society, Washington, D.C.

"Pea, n" *Oxford English Dictionary* online. Accessed 11/23/15.

Simpson, B.B. and M. C. Orgazaly. 2014. *Economic Botany*. 4th ed. McGraw-Hill, New York.

van Wyk, B-E. 2005. *Food Plants of the World*. Timber Press, Portland. OR.

Vaughan, J. G. and C. Geissler. 1997. *The New Oxford Book of Food Plants*. Oxford University Press, Oxford.

Vickery, R. 1997. *The Oxford Dictionary of Plant-Lore*. Oxford University Press, Oxford.

Last Words

GARDEN PLANTS ARE ALL AROUND US, whether we garden or just walk through public places.

But they weren't always where they are today. Most garden plants have had centuries of being grown by people. In that time they picked up folklore and traveled great distances, leading to wonderful stories. These stories tell us about plants but they tell us more about ourselves.

Beautiful plants were used in very different cultures around the world. Tasty plants may have been equally loved by diverse peoples, but eaten in quite different ways. We create mythological origins for the plants and decide some plants are lucky and others unlucky. When technology changes, hard-to-preserve vegetables become widely eaten while crop weeds might be driven to local extinction.

The plants we grow and love change over time and are subject to fads. Styles change and an new flower replaces the old familiar ones. That change may be slow or very sudden. All our common plants have pasts where they might have been known by another name or been used quite differently. Sometimes learning the history of a plant suddenly explains something you had observed, but always those stories entertain.

Best of all, it is an ongoing story. Each of us meets the plants anew and shapes our garden encounters for ourselves.

Of course, what I said above applies beyond garden plants. Read about some of them in my book, *Curious Stories of Familiar Plants*, and check out other stories on:
My website: **www.AWanderingBotanist.com**
My blog: **www.KHKeeler.Blogspot.com**.

Wherever you go, notice the plants!

A Wandering Botanist visits Australia.

www.ingramcontent.com/pod-product-compliance
Lightning Source LLC
Chambersburg PA
CBHW042337150426
43195CB00001B/25